Shine:
A Pleadean Message to Awaken Your True Purpose and Power

ELSABE SMIT

Cover: Terri Radcliffe at brandrepublica.com

ISBN: 1539079392
ISBN-13: 978-1539079392

CONTENTS

FAITH AND TRUST

I have been hesitant to go along this route for a few years now, but I have reached a point where I feel obliged to do what I have to do.

During 2012 and 2013 I received very interesting messages from entities that tell me they are from the Pleiades. The information still makes so much sense that I have no problem signing my name next to the messages. I have published an entire book on the topic of healing (*Deep Blue: A Guide to Empowerment Healing* - refer to the back of this book for details), the origins of which will make an interesting story, and which comes from the same source.

Here goes:

1 RADIO SIGNALS

You already understand about the magnetic charges of the planets. But there is more to it.

The analogy of radio signals will do. As we get closer to the change (21st December 2012), the reception that you and many other people have will become clearer. Your telepathic powers will increase to a point where speech will become redundant.

For you this will happen in your lifetime. This is not due to a change in your DNA – that is hype.

The change is happening exactly because of what you so eloquently describe – you are removing all the 'white noise' so that your reception will become clearer.

You have mastered your thinking process to the level where what you say becomes. Your dreams are materializing because you no longer have any obstacles left.

You have grown to the point where you are becoming aware of obstacles before they are fully formed, and you dissolve them quicker than ever before.

The process that you have documented is nearly perfect. We will provide you with more information on how you can access the quantum vibration at will.

Of course, this will allow you to materialize your thoughts at will. However, we will for the moment retain control of what you materialize.

We do trust your intentions and abilities. We want to use you to achieve our objectives sooner. Once we have the basis in place, we will give you full control of these powers.

You are overcoming the last resistance to the flow and the process.

We are also removing the last hindrances and the last control over time.

Your timelines will speed up and you will see changes happening faster.

We are also removing some pedantic elements of your life, so that the energy flow will become purer and faster.

You will soon experience an increase in your healing powers. You will also have flashes of insight. We want you to record and communicate these insights. There is an entire audience ready and waiting. Do not hesitate and wonder about those who are not in the audience yet.

Forge ahead. We will guide you. Blessed be.

2 HEALING

Much has been said and written about healing in the past few hundred years. Most of it just scratched the surface and were based on speculation.

Progress in earth science has led to much more speculation. The time has come to open a new layer of knowledge. People are not ready yet to uncover the full truth about healing, no matter how joyful and powerful it is.

The earth is no longer fit to be inhabited by people and at the same time humanity has progressed to the next level of evolution.

There will be much conflict over the next few years because of this situation. Some people will blame others for abusing the earth and its resources. We do not deny that the earth has in places been abused, but that is not the sole reason why it is time for the earth to be vacated.

As the human race progressed through the ages - as with any other progression - layers were formed. The top layer, if we can call it that, is ready for the next level of evolution. This next level cannot take place on earth, because there are too many restrictions even in the most open minds.

The most restrictive thoughts relate to time and space. There are many levels of evolution yet to come for humanity. The next level takes place outside of time and space.

Much of the current and impending conflict between people relates to fear and a desire to cling to time and space, because people believe that is all there is.

They do not see experiences such as dreams and daydreams as proof that time and space are superfluous.

More and more regulation and legislation are brought in to regulate people's thoughts. This has become frantic and frankly laughable.

The pendulum is slowly swinging to where anarchy will rule because people no longer want to distinguish between useful and useless rules. Their solution is to throw out all rules even when they are not ready yet to listen to their inner voice and follow their own sensible thoughts.

We will give more information and guidance in a series of articles, describing how to manage this transition to the next level of evolution.

Blessed be.

3 A NEW HUMAN RACE

Blessed be. This is a message from the Pleiades to people of the earth. You are living in challenging times because the changes have not been completed yet.

A new human race is being born. We are not only referring to babies and small children with heightened intuitive abilities. We are talking about people of all ages who have awakened to their spirit, and whose physical bodies have been adapted to follow suit.

We will not go into the technicalities of this physical adaptation. Suffice to say that people cannot pay for any course, workshop or expert to obtain this adaptation or an imitation of it.

Those people whose bodies have been adapted after they have received the calling are aware of what has happened to them.

They have naturally withdrawn from using mind-altering substances such as alcohol and medication. They have made intuitive changes to their diets - and these changes are individual. There are no rules such as excluding meat or eating only organic foods.

The adapted bodies can live on any food that they choose, even food with added chemicals, because their bodies cleanse the food.

These chosen people - and there is no magic number of them - know that they have received our calling because they have slowed down and softened their approach to the world. They are truly now 'in this world but not of this world'.

Over time these people will naturally be drawn to each other. Their individual strength will be grouped together and therein lies their power.

Yes, there will still be conflict because much work is not completed yet, but that is natural and part of the process.

Blessed be.

5

4 RELIGION AND EXCLUSIVITY

This is a message for all those people who believe in exclusivity. We are referring to religious people who believe only their religion is true. We are also referring to people who believe that no religion is true, because that is also a form of exclusivity if you want to exclude people from what is known as spirituality because they have religious beliefs. All of these beliefs are incomplete spirals.

When you accept that there will always be religious groups as long as people inhabit the earth, you are halfway there.

Accepting each one of those religions with everything they encompass will place you above exclusivity.

Accept that all religions have inherent forms of violence. Even if the violence is not physical, it is still there. Do not judge the violence. Accept it as part of the human condition.

Even the saintliest non-religious person has violence in them. To deny that is to judge, and to judge is to discover another spiral you need to complete.

Accept.

5 ASPECTS OF LOVE 1

We want to explain some of the intricacies of Love. So many people are looking for Love, and will sacrifice anything to be in a loving relationship.

Love does not require sacrifice in any form. The thought of Love being proven by means of sacrifice was planted in the human psyche thousands of years ago, as part of a manipulation that had nothing to do with Love.

Yes, you are thinking about Abraham and his son, Isaac. That had nothing to do with Love. We repeat: Love does not require sacrifice in any form.

Now go and consider all those Love relationships where you feel you sacrifice, and ask yourself how much Love will remain when you stop sacrificing. Every answer will bring you closer to self-Love. When you have self-Love, you are closer to understanding Love.

6 CONSISTENCY

Why does the sun keep shining? Because there is consistency. The sun will keep shining for a few million years to come.

In the same way, your behavior is consistent and will continue. We want to take your consistency to a much higher level in this explanation.

Of course, your behavior is consistent in the sense that you get up every morning and go to work, and so on. Or if you are not employed, you still have your daily routine and expectations.

This is not the consistency we are referring to.

You know that your life and routine is disrupted by small or larger conflict all the time. Sometimes this conflict is resolved quickly, and at other times the conflict can drag on for months and even years before it is resolved. However, the conflict is consistently resolved and that is what we want to bring to your attention.

Your purpose on this earth is to experience and resolve conflict. And no, we are not war-mongers – there are enough of them on this earth already. We do not refer to conflict with other people. Our focus is on helping you resolve inner conflict that is reflected in the world that you live in. We manage the process that helps you resolve your own inner conflict.

Everything begins and ends with you, and you represent humanity. This is the case no matter how big or small you are, no matter how important or insignificant you deem yourself, no matter how you see yourself in relation to other people.

You are not only your brother's keeper. You are your brother.

Where you cannot love your neighbor (yes, we have also read that book), you cannot love yourself. That is the conflict that will always be resolved, and that is the consistency that we are referring to.

Love yourself, and you love the entire Universe.

7 BREATHING

Today we want to explain the nature of breathing - and no, this is not a lesson in biology.

Breathing is of course a chemical process, because it sustains the body.

However, there is a philosophical aspect to breathing that you need to understand.

Breathing is about giving life. With your first in-breath as a new-born baby you receive the gift of life. We will not discuss the life of a fetus - we leave that for another day.

Your gift of life continues until you leave this existence. Every in-breath is a new gift.

Is your out-breath then not a gift? Yes, it also is, because it allows you to leave behind substances that are contrary to life. Every out-breath is a cleansing exercise.

This is not a yogic gimmick. This is ancient knowledge that we want to bring to the forefront of consciousness.

People in modern civilization have forgotten how to breathe. They express gratitude for tangible things, but forget to use the gift of life.

Be conscious of every breath you take today.

8 WHO IS YOUR NEIGHBOUR?

What does loving your neighbor mean? And who is your neighbor? This is another aspect of Love that we want to explain.

Your neighbor is really everyone on this planet, including tyrants, fraudsters, philosophers, bigamists - no matter how you want to label them.

Loving everyone on the planet is an easy task - as is proven by politicians all the time. Loving your neighbor is much more complex, because your neighbor includes family members, friends, the trouble-makers in your community and even your own body.

Here is your task for today: make a list of the people that you find difficult to Love, even though you know you are obliged to. Make a list of the people you Love but don't like right now.

What do all these people have in common? You. If anybody needs to change, you do.

How do you need to change? Ask yourself why you do not Love these people. In what way do you judge them? Then work on acceptance. Accept them as being different from you, and therefore complementing you. They will not change. You will need to change your view of them.

No, you do not need to do this all at once. Do it for one person at a time, and see how your Love grows.

You are blessed.

9 THE NATURE OF LIGHT

Our topic for today is Light. Every person on earth is a source of Light. Yes, even the person with the darkest heart is a source of Light. For this person, the Light may not be that visible and their aura may reflect darkness, but even darkness cannot be reflected without Light.

This is not a lecture about shining your Light in the world. This is providing you with information about your life purpose.

Every person is a divided being. This is reflected in the amount of conflict on earth.

We are here to help you focus on finding inner peace. And no, that is not a cliché. Inner peace is a result of resolving inner conflict.

Whenever you make peace with a part of yourself, that part of yourself turns into Light, and you become both lighter and more visible in the world.

Your life purpose is to strive towards resolving all the inner conflict that you chose to carry into this existence.

As you do this, you become more whole and you get closer to being a Light being.

How can you hasten the process? By acknowledging your inner conflict and working towards resolving it.

And yes, you have to resolve the conflict because it is your conflict and your division.

Blessings to you.

10 QUESTION YOUR FAITH

Today we want to get straight into the nitty gritty of faith. Every person on this planet has faith, even if it is only faith in this life or in themselves and nothing else.

Our purpose is not to convert a planet, because each one of these faiths was at some stage required to get humanity where they are.

We offer an inclusive alternative based on Love and Light.

What will happen when people do not accept this alternative? They will get on with their lives.

And what will happen with people do accept our message? They will still get on with their lives.

However, they will ask those questions that their faith does not allow them to ask. They will get honest answers and clarity without fear.

Any faith based on fear needs to be questioned. We do not bring judgement and retribution. We bring Love and Light. We bring information that result in unity and healing.

Yes, you will see much healing in the coming years, and much of this healing will be inexplicable in the current medical paradigm. But we will be able to explain every step of the way, and only those who are willing to accept our message will understand.

We will leave you to think about this.

11 OUR COLOURFUL SPIRITS

Have you noticed how color determines your mood? Have you noticed how you shy away from colors that you are not at peace with? And how you are attracted to colors that tell the world about you?

No, you do not need to like and use all colors. But be aware of the message you give to the world by the colors you use and wear. Too much color also creates a confusing message.

What does color have to do with your beliefs and faith, you may ask? Let us explain.

Everything in this world is an expression of spirit - your spirit. We used colors to start the message, but we could easily have used sound, crimes, books, drugs or anything else to convey the same message.

We will tell you more and more often to be aware. Be aware of your thoughts, words and actions, because they shape your world. The first step towards change is not to change, but to be aware of yourself. Your awareness starts today.

12 THE PUREST FORM OF ENERGY

Today we have much to say but it is necessary. There has been much talk over the last century about energy conservation. We have seen some strange schemes and concepts to "green the earth" and "generate new sources of energy". Most of these have amused us, and some have concerned us. It is time to give you a new perspective.

Energy cannot be generated, created or re-created. All the energy that is in this world is here to stay as long as people inhabit the earth, and the energy will remain when the last person leaves. Yes, the earth will eventually be vacated, but there is no need to start packing yet. This message will form part of history long after all current readers have gone.

So, what should be done about energy? Of course, we cannot stop schemes related to reducing carbon or generating wind or any other interesting inventions.

But we can guide you towards the cleanest, clearest, purest form of energy that you can control. You.

Yes, that is not a typing error. You are all the energy you will ever need.

We are at the dawn of an era where people are developing their personal energy to its limit.

You will experience an expansion of your intuitive abilities, but that is not all.

You will in the next few generations experience creations that will astonish and change the world - and we are pleased to say that these creations will be for the benefit of earth and all its inhabitants.

Most of these new creations will be so simple that they will be regarded as primitive. They will become fashion accessories and then they will become part of daily life.

There is a new generation of children who will take the lead on this.

These children will suffer all sorts of labels because of their social behavior and they will be described as 'rebels' and 'uncontrollable' but they will have the purity that is required of future leaders.

They will only be regarded as 'uncontrollable' because they question all constructs that are not pure, and they do not hesitate to cause conflict to remove these impure constructs.

You wonder whether we are judgmental when we describe things or ideas as impure?

We do not attach any emotion to the words, because we have no use for emotions. We compare what is on the earth to what will be in the future and eternity. That is our definition of 'impure'. We will take humanity back to the energy of new-born babies who know no judgement.

The next few centuries will make interesting history.

13 A TURNING POINT

Today is a turning point for many people. This is an astrologically significant day for the earth. You do not need to know the details of the planets, and no astrologer on earth has the full picture to give the explanation. But we can tell you that your Universe, and by default all its inhabitants, have turned today.

We like your questioning nature because it helps others to also get clarity.

You are asking about the fluid nature of time and how a single day can be of any significance.

Yes, time is fluid when applied to all human emotional experiences. You know from experience that events related to people can seldom be predicted to the day, unless there is a conscious decision that involves more than one person. For example, you can predict that thousands of people will go to work next Monday, but you can only give an estimation as to when each of them will resolve their own inner conflict.

The astrological event of today is a confluence of energy that forms part of a much greater scheme that is not controlled by the inhabitants of Earth.

You are experiencing the effect of the event. For some people it will feel like darkness descending, because they are on the ascent. For other people it will feel like Light finally arriving, and they are ready to enter through the portal.

And no, there is space for everyone. All people will eventually step through the portal - not only the first 144 000.

What do you need to do about this day? Continue doing what you are doing. Either be ready for the ascent or be ready to step through the portal. You know where you are today.

Keep striving until you can fully feel and acknowledge the Light within. That Light is always there and your journey is about realizing it.

Blessings to you and have a happy journey.

14 ETERNITY

Today we will explain Eternity to you. No, we will not enter a diatribe about life and death.

Eternity is much more than just about an earthly transition and change in energy.

Eternity is where you come from, where you are and where you are going. Yes, we do check our grammar - please do not consider changing our words.

There are religious groups that want to separate life here from Eternity. That would be like separating chocolate beans from chocolate and still calling the result chocolate.

Life on this earth and in this body is merely a different journey during a journey with no beginning and no end.

Only the inhabitants of earth attach so much value to the human body. On other planets where there is life the body is a vessel and respected as a separate citizen.

The journey is not about the physical body and about superficial agendas like age, gender or skin color. Those are just attributes or aspects of the inner conflict that you all came to resolve.

When you leave your body, you realize how superficial much of this journey is. But we are not discarding the meaning of your journey on earth. We are placing it into perspective - the perspective of Eternity.

Ask yourself on your journey today how important your little irritations really are. See them as the proverbial grains of sand on the beach of the Universe, which is a grain of sand in Eternity.

We do understand that the purpose of your journey is to resolve inner conflict. But we are asking you to focus on that real conflict and not be distracted by superficial aspects that are not real.

Blessings to you.

15 PATIENCE

Today's message is about patience - and it is meant for you and the world.

There are many preachers who tell you that you can have everything you want, and they have all sorts of secret recipes and techniques to help you address your 'failures'.

None of those techniques contain the whole truth.

The process of creation is a result of inner growth. The more you grow, the more creative you become. And the more creative you are, the more you grow.

Of course, we measure creativity in the beauty you create with your actions.

Where does patience come into this? When you want something to happen or materialize, no technique in the world will help you to get or experience it before you are ready.

How do you get ready for the future? That is easy. Live today to the fullest and do not discard your creations from yesterday. The more you live in the future, the more patience you need today.

See yourself as part of a massive puzzle. As long as you are a lone piece, there is no picture. You can only form part of the picture when all the pieces are in place. Have patience, and all will fall into place for you.

You are Loved.

16 ACCEPT YOUR 'KILLER SIDE'

Do we have a cracking message for you!

Do you remember the legend of the great flood? No, this is not a warning of another flood to come. And yes, of course that is more than a legend - the flood was real.

Before the flood happened there was enough warning. And yes, there was enough meteorological knowledge available. Your current civilization is not unique.

You are now experiencing conditions similar to the great flood. We are referring not only to weather patterns, but also to social patterns. And yes, you have advanced in many ways socially, but humanity has also come full circle.

The sad thing is that the same cleansing is now taking place - with no help from nature this time. People are destroying people.

But as with everything in this Universe and in Eternity, there is balance. For every person that is physically killed, another person is spiritually born. We are not talking about an increase in population. We are talking about a change in energy.

There is no reason for people to keep killing each other so that the spiritual change can continue.

The earth will eventually be vacated, whether people kill each other or not.

So rather than kill another person or kill yourself, why not accept your 'killer side'?

A wise man once referred to the two tigers in you - the protective one and the attacking one. Which one is the strongest? The one that you feed!

The earth will be vacated, but not in the next few generations. Humanity is not ready to move on yet.

Focus on your inner conflict today and choose which one you feed. Blessings to you.

17 BALANCE AND PEACE

Today - in fact, any day - is an appropriate time to talk about balance. As you have already gathered, the Universe - yours as well as others - is in complete balance. This balance goes wider than just your known Universe. There is another Universe, much like yours, where your opposites reign. Believe us - you would rather be in your Universe.

This balance reigns not only on the largest scale, but also on the smallest scale - in the cells of your body. There is a beautiful symphony that plays between you and your body all the time. The more you gain control over your emotions, the more you hear the symphony.

For everything that dies, something new is born. What is born is not necessarily visible, and neither is what dies. Even with what is visible, people tend to overlook it.

Look at your life. What have you gained? At what price? What have you lost? And how much did you gain from that loss? Find your balance and find your peace.

Blessings to you.

18 THE DAY OF JUDGMENT

Today is a day of retribution - but so is every day. You create your own retribution when you measure what you have achieved against your dreams and potential.

This is a short message.

Do you really want to hand out retribution to others before you are done with yourself? Take some time to recollect your dreams. What are you doing about them?

When you achieve your own dreams. you make the world a better place for others. This is the true ripple effect.

You are blessed.

19 THE NATURE OF TIME

Let us explain the nature of time. Time is a measurement, but it is just that. It is a dimension like the more physical length, breadth and height, but it is still only a measurement of the core, which is the truth.

What is far more important is timing, when another cycle of oneness is completed.

You may have noticed that some people hold on to their emotions like grief and hatred for a long time. That is because they are not ready to let go as long as those emotions serve a purpose for them.

It does not matter how many weeks or months pass, or how many full moons come and go. If only it were as easy as that, many psychologists and therapists will go out of business.

The measurement of your truth is about timing - about when you are ready to let go of your emotions.

You will know that the timing is right because you will be ready to experience gratitude and forgiveness.

So, stop asking 'When will it happen?' but rather ask 'When will I be ready to accept?' and don't expect an answer.

May your blessings multiply.

20 TIME IS AN ILLUSION

We need to correct a misconception. Time does not stand still - ever. Time also does not move - and it especially does not fly.

Time is an illusion - a very strong one that people have bought into to the extent that it causes much stress.

Everything you do seems to be time-bound - even a meditation is timed.

There will come a time when such an artificial limitation will fall away. For now, it is necessary for people to experience the destructive element of time, because it helps to condense conflict and enhances the process of becoming whole.

Use your time, but do not become a slave of it. You do not want to be the slave of an illusion.

Do not focus on how much you can achieve within a given time. Rather focus on savoring the moment - even if it is a stressful moment, because that will help you appreciate a stress-less moment. As we have taught you, balance is everything.

Have you noticed how you can have a good or a bad time? On that level, you recognize time as a label rather than a dimension.

Timing is fluid and far more meaningful than time.

Love and Blessings to you.

21 THE MAGNIFICENT UNIVERSE

Goodness, you are the most reluctant messenger we have ever had. You should know by now that you can trust us.

We want to remind you of the magnificence of the Universe that you live in. The whole purpose of your Universe initially was to be a testing ground for a new breed. The experiment has succeeded and we are satisfied.

That is why in another seven generations the earth will be mostly evacuated.

This evacuation will be voluntary, non-violent and a result of further refinement in spirit.

The organisms that form your body will travel with you to the new destination, but they will no longer form the unit that lives with your soul and spirit.

Yes, your soul is different from your spirit. That is a quantum physical explanation that we will leave for later.

We will leave you to digest this.

Blessings to you.

22 FOLLOW YOUR DESTINY

Today we want to sound like those motivational teachers who say 'never give up'.

The difference is that they look at man-made goals, whereas we look at destiny.

There is nothing wrong with man-made goals. They are necessary like mass-manufactured dresses have a place. We deal, in a manner of speaking, with the designer talent.

Once you have an inkling of your destiny, follow that inkling. You know the difference between a wish and a deep sense of knowing, as you call it. Follow your deep sense of knowing and never waver. We are in the background, creating the stage for what is your destiny. You are the one who has to walk onto that stage.

And your stage, Elsabe, is not just a proverbial one. You will be on a stage soon, fulfilling your destiny. We are right behind you. Never give up.

Blessings to all of you.

23 THE NATURE OF FORGIVENESS

Remember, your thoughts create your future.

Today we want to talk to you about forgiveness.

Do you really think we would leave anything as important as forgiveness in the hands of people to apply the way they think they can?

Please focus here.

Forgiveness is not about absolving another person. In fact, we will leave the definition of forgiveness for another day.

Let us rather focus on why you take the actions that determine the main course of your life.

You have access to cellular memory - not in your physical body but in your ethereal body that travels with you.

That memory dictates your past, present and future actions. No, the memory is not time-bound. The memory reminds you of contracts with other people and steers your actions. The overall purpose of your memory is to help you integrate your inner conflict and become whole.

This means you can stop blaming yourself for your past actions, and see how they have made you whole.

If you can do that, how can other people help you by forgiving you?

They cannot - they are merely co-actors on the stage of life.

At the same time, you cannot help others by forgiving them.

Rather focus on how your actions and experiences make you whole. That brings you closer to forgiveness, which we will explain later. (Refer chapter 41)

24 THE WORKINGS OF WATER

Today we want to get technical. We want to explain to you the workings of water.

You are already aware of the uniqueness of water as a fluid that can take different shapes. You already know that water contains communication. How do you listen to those communications? By taking in the purest water you can get.

Once the water enters your body, the communication starts. Your body cells absorb the water and the messages go from your body cells to your brain.

Water always has a purifying action. You need to take in as much water every day as you feel comfortable with. Listen to your body. And take in water, not diluted water. In fact, there is no such thing as diluted water. You use water to dilute other substances. When you do that, the message from the water is put aside and the energy of the water focuses on cleansing the substance. Rather take in pure water and get a pure message. Try it and feel the difference.

And of course, blessings to you.

25 TRUE POWER

We want to explain true power to you. There are many powerful people in your world. That is what most of them are - full of power. Then there are a handful of world leaders, ordinary people, artists, writers, healers - of every label you can conceive of - who understand the meaning of true power and who use their power to help others.

You need to know that not everyone who helps others has true power. Sadly, most people in the helping industry get their power from the people they help. Yes, we understand that you are brave to take out to the world a message that may offend people. We are here to deliver the truth.

True power does not lie in how many people have faith in you and give their power to you. That is the greatest fake power there is, and the best example is politicians who in themselves have very little power, but then they become power-full by robbing people of their power.

True power lies in those individuals who give hope to the world, no matter what happens. They often 'swim upstream' - they are often loners who follow their calling and flout the rules made by power-full people. They expose the flaws, even at a cost to themselves.

You could keep and grow your own power by questioning your own actions. Do you give power away to others? Do you take power from others? Focus your own power on becoming the person you are meant to become.

Blessings to you.

26 NEW-NESS

Today we have a message of new-ness to you. Yes, we know that is a different way of using language and we are doing it on purpose.

New-ness is an attribute of what you have not experienced yet. We want to explain this without becoming too scientific.

When you have a new experience, the neurons in your brain connect in a different way. This is like wandering through familiar territory and then deciding to explore a new path. There is a short moment of initial excitement, followed by a split second decision.

When the new-ness is not much different from familiar experiences, the decision is often to continue and accept the new-ness, which then becomes familiar.

When the new-ness pushes boundaries, the initial excitement creates other emotions that make the new experience more challenging. When this happens, the choice to remain behind or move forward becomes conscious.

If you then decide not to accept the new-ness, you create a block in the flow of your energy.

You are asking where free will fits into this?

We are explaining free will. You can accept or decline the new-ness. And yes, when you decline the new-ness, you create an energy block. The new-ness was created as part of your path to ensure the continuous flow of energy.

By you choosing to decline the new-ness, you choose the energy blockage.

Not all new experiences provide the same level of challenge.

When you accept the challenge your level of vibration increases. You experience inner peace at a higher level.

Accept the new-ness that comes to you today and understand that it is necessary for your growth.

Blessings to you.

27 TOLERANCE

Today we want to talk to you about tolerance. There is so much intolerance in this world, starting with traffic and going right up to world wars about things that should unite rather than divide people.

Why are people so intolerant?

Because they do not see the wonder of variety! They do not understand that when they push away opposites, they in fact attract those opposites to them.

We are not talking about any law of this or law of that.

We are talking about what you on earth like to call quantum physics. Oh, and thank you for using our words – we know you are sometimes tempted to use your own.

Yes, we do talk about opposites attracting. That is the path to one-ness, which is your mission on earth.

Tolerance does not mean becoming what you abhor. It means accepting what you are, and therefore accepting what others are – especially when they are different from you. You do not need to lose or give anything away. All you need to do is accept those that are different from you. Accept that you cannot change their choices.

Wars are being fought about one group wanting another group to accept their culture and habits. People fight and resist when in fact they need to learn and accept.

Yes, we know you are thinking about women being oppressed and children being abused. There is a fine line between helping them overcome their circumstances and being intolerant of their choices.

Go and think about this: the world starts to change with your next breath, not with your next action. Judgement and justice are the opposite of tolerance.

Blessings to you all.

28 ACCEPTANCE

Today we want to talk about acceptance. And no, acceptance is not about being a doormat and allowing people to step on you. In a situation like that acceptance comes from understanding why you allow it, and then changing if you want it.

This kind of acceptance – the only true kind – applies to all situations, whether you label them to be good or bad.

All situations happen because you and your co-actors create them. The situations are meant to be there to help you achieve one-ness. When you have achieved the one-ness of the situation you understand why the situations occur. That understanding is followed by acceptance of the learning, the teaching, the lesson – whatever you want to call it. We see it as achieving one-ness.

Go and think about it. What situation are you allowing to drag on because you have not reached that one-ness and acceptance yet? And you will discover that other people involved in the situation either have reached their one-ness and accepted and moved on, or they are at various stages of conflict and heading for the pinnacle, the one-ness and the acceptance.

When all is said and done, you are a bundle of nerves in a state. Are you nerves in a state of equilibrium or exhaustion? If you feel exhaustion, let go and let God. That is one-ness and acceptance.

Have a blessed day.

29 A WORLD AT WAR

Today we have an important message that must be spread widely. This is about war. The world is slowly steering towards another wide war that we cannot avoid, no matter what we do.

You are asking about our powers? Believe it or not, we cannot change the course of the world. We can provide this and other information to you and other people like you. But we cannot make anyone change their course. Everything that happens on earth is part of the journey towards one-ness.

That is why we cannot prevent any war. We can ask you to help make people aware. The awareness will speed up the process towards one-ness.

Every person who awakens and realizes what their choice is can and will move closer to acceptance, tolerance and one-ness, and away from war.

Rejection and intolerance comes from not recognizing that your neighbor is part of you.

Now that the world is described as a global village it is so much easier to understand that your neighbor can live on the other side of the world and still be your neighbor.

War is not necessary and can be avoided if every person recognizes the daily war inside of themselves. That is a war you can win by knowing your emotions and moving towards one-ness. Every step towards acceptance takes you away from war with others.

Blessed be.

30 INFINITY

Today we want to explain infinity. It will be a short explanation.

Infinity is everything and nothing. Infinity is who you are.

Would you like to experience infinity? Physically it is not possible because you will need to stop breathing.

Does that mean that infinity is nothing and there is nothing after physical death? Not at all! Yes, it is like nothing you have experienced in this life.

The closest you will get to infinity is when you go into a deep meditation, where you cannot stop breathing and you cannot stop your skin from sensing.

Why do you need to know about this?

Because infinity is also everything.

You have the capacity to create anything you want simply by fetching it from infinity.

You may want to ask why people fetch horrendous experiences when they can focus on creating.

When you accept your own power, you are ready to create your own presence and future. When you are afraid of your own power, you allow other people to create your present and future.

Sadly, you humans have created cultures that create and fester fear.

Fear is the opposite of power. Once you are ready to create power, you will no longer want fear.

Once you have experienced fear, you are ready to create power and use it.

We are not talking about power based on your own fears or on the fears of others. That is not power, but rather a pretense of power.

True power does not cause pain or fear for anyone. True power is pure joy. You will soon experience true power. Humanity is blessed.

31 TURMOIL AND TORMENT

Today we want to talk about turmoil and torment. We love the sound of that - not only because of all the t's in it but also because turmoil and torment comes right before gratitude.

You and your readers (and we love them all) know how the period before gratitude is always the most difficult.

You are familiar with those nights when you toss and turn, and no matter how you practice all sorts of techniques, you cannot still your thoughts.

You know about the long, imaginary conversations you have with the people who cause your turmoil and torment.

We are not offering a magic alternative. We are offering understanding. When you have those moments, do not try to suppress them and become holier than thou. Rather be aware of what is happening - both in your life and in your mind.

Those thoughts will always run their course. They will recede by themselves as the conversation in your mind dies down. That is part of the process.

You know the process already. We do hear some of your readers asking for details of the process.

We intend to dictate an entire book to you that will clarify it all. Put that also on your to-do-list.

For now, allow those thoughts to die down on their own. Don't let the thoughts consume you, because those thoughts are not you. Those thoughts are like ribbons in your hair. When you remove the ribbons, your hair remains. Those thoughts are like ribbons that fall out once they have served their purpose. Then your hair becomes your crowning glory again.

You ask how this message applies to bald people? Remember, they also had hair, and they always have imagination.

So, go and resolve your turmoil and torment, and experience gratitude and peace.

Blessings to you.

32 CLOUDS OF DOUBT

Let's talk about clouds for a minute. Yes, a minute, not a moment. You heard right. Put those barriers aside. We have never misled you and we never will.

We want to explain the clouds of doubt that even the strongest believers have- and we are talking about all people who strongly believe in anything, whether it is spiritual, mechanical, religious, scientific or anything else.

Yes, those clouds serve a purpose. This is how it works: you start at the point where the belief is not relevant to you, but then it gets challenged. You then start to defend your belief, which grows stronger – but so does the challenge.

That is where your clouds of doubt appear. You fully accept your belief, but you also cannot ignore the challenge. Therefore, you do nothing, and wait for the clouds to settle.

During this time, you feel lost – adrift – even a traitor to yourself.

But when those clouds open, you have total clarity. You understand clearly why you had the doubts, and how you will move forward. Looking back, the resolution of the doubts becomes a solid part of your foundation. You move from being a student to being a teacher.

And then you see the clouds in other people's minds. You understand their doubts. You are able to help them step by step, at their own pace, through the clouds, because you have been there and risen above the clouds. And at the same time your level of skill has grown.

You experience this all the time in different areas of your life and it is a natural process. You could beat yourself up about having doubts, or you could see your truth unfold and see a miracle happening.

Be good to yourself and blessings to you.

33 POLITICS

Today we want to explain the role of politics. Yes, politicians are often reviled, but they do play an important role. They are the barometer of the society you created. When they lie, it is because they conform to the norm. When they don't care, it is because they conform to the norm everyone created.

When they support causes, it is because they can see some benefit in the causes. And they do it for the people. They are an excellent barometer, but that is hardly ever noticed. They are seen as 'the other'.

How do you deal with this? You do not suddenly all get involved in politics - that would be even more chaotic than your world already is.

You do study the politicians and their utterances. Then you identify the part of your life that reflects them. They you decide what you want to do about that.

If you want to accept that part of you, then do so. If you want to change that part of you, then first accept it, because acceptance is the basis of change. It you want to reject that part of you, then ask yourself why. This is important, because you cannot reject a part of you, just like your right arm will not go away if you choose to reject it.

The only way you can change the world is by becoming consciously more aware of the world and accepting yourself and your part in it. That will allow you the choice of accepting or rejecting and making an informed choice.

Go and study those politicians - they are a good barometer at all times.

Blessings to you.

34 WHEN DO YOU HELP?

Today we want to talk to you about empathy. At what point does empathy stop and good deeds begin? And yes, we want to say 'good' deeds, because that judgement is in the eye of the beholder.

You have asked before when is it right to change the course of another person's life.

The answer to that is simple - you never do. Each person makes their own choices all the time - and that includes the hungry children in Africa. They are, like you, a spirit inhabiting a body while on their own journey.

So how can you help them? Where does empathy stop and action begin? If you ever have to ask the question, then the action will be to interfere with the life choices of others.

We are not saying you must never help other people - on the contrary.

Your heart will tell you when to help another person, and you will intuitively do it long before your mind catches up.

When your mind tells you what to do, it is time for you to question your own motives. When you act on what your mind wants, you will expect payback and reward and recognition.

Always listen first to your heart. Your mind has its own lessons to learn. One of them is that there is a difference between empathy and Love.

Blessings to you.

35 HOW TO DEAL WITH NOISY NEIGHBOURS

Love your neighbors. Yes, we have explained this before, but we will have to do it a few more times.

Loving your neighbor does not mean being overly tolerant or being judgmental. If your neighbor makes your life hell, then you have to change. That's right, you have to change, not your neighbor.

Let's say, for example, that your neighbors are very noisy. Do you fight with them all the time? No. They are already inconsiderate, and fighting will make no difference.

So, what do you do? You accept that you cannot change them.

Once you have accepted that, you reach a state of equilibrium.

Your neighbors will still be noisy. The difference will be in the energy that radiates from you. You will no longer react from emotion, but act from authority.

Your neighbors will become aware of this change even before you tell them. They will calm down. And if they still don't, any steps you take from that position of authority will reach them and cause them to tone down.

Will they ever be only considerate? Can you push back the west wind? No. But you can move out and leave a legacy. Once people change to a higher level of vibration, they do not change back. The same happens to your neighbors. If that is the only role you play in their lives, it is a significant role.

Now go and love your neighbors.

36 BELIEFS AND FAITH

You are quite a challenge for us, because you are such a mixture of belief and non-belief. One day there will only be belief. In the meantime, we enjoy and love working with you. We will never disappoint you.

Today's topic is ... beliefs. Yes, there is a difference between faith and beliefs. Take yourself for example. You have lost and gained many beliefs during your life. You have seen other people become disillusioned.

You have learned to distinguish between our instructions and your thoughts.

And underneath all of these happenings your faith has grown and it is strong as ever.

That is the difference between faith and beliefs. Beliefs change based on your life experiences.

Faith is like a beacon that always guides you, always there, even when you are at the beginning or end of a life cycle.

Beliefs may fail you, but faith is always there.

Beliefs are the obstacles that you need to overcome, so as to strengthen your faith.

We bless you.

37 RUNNING OUT OF FAITH

We have a little message for you about running out of faith. That is not possible.

Faith is like water. Even when you think there is none left, you still have water in your body, and then it rains.

Blessings to you.

38 BEING RE-BORN

A new life is not limited to birth – it starts every day. All of you are re-born every day. All of you are re-born every day, with new Love, new opportunities and everything new.

Then why do you not see much of the new life every day? Because too often you drag yesterday with you, while you are running towards tomorrow.

Take a deep breath today and remember this day for the rest of your life.

It is a day on which everything changes.

Blessings and Love to you.

39 DOING GOOD DEEDS

This message is about doing good deeds. So often people do deeds which they believe to show themselves as good people, and which they believe to be in the interest of others.

Any deeds that come from that place do neither good nor bad. Those deeds disturb the process of growth, because they come straight from the mind. Real good deeds require no contemplation.

Remember that.

Be blessed.

40 BROTHERLY LOVE

We have a message for humanity today. This is about brotherly Love.

Yes, we do understand that brotherly love is impossible to understand when people kill, maim, hurt and injure each other for no reason.

But let us explain it in this way.

When you cook beans without water or any other fluid, you don't cook at all – you just burn the food. The moment you add water, you retain the fluids and you can eat the food with its nutrients.

Every person on this planet responds to Love.

When a person has never felt Love before, or when they have felt and lost the Love, they are like beans on an open fire. That is when they most need Love, not judgement.

We know that this sounds harsh to people who have never thought that Love can cure everything, but Love can and does cure everything – whether the person kills one or two or seventy-eight people.

Just like nobody is ever beyond redemption, nobody is ever beyond Love.

Imagine a legal system that exposes people to Love rather than judgment. Now that will change the world.

And you can start this on a small scale, by simply sending memories of the Love you have personally experienced to the person you otherwise would have judged.

Much Love to you.

41 FORGIVENESS AND UNDERSTANDING

We have a message for humanity – about forgiveness. Much damage has been done with the concept of turning the other cheek, and much dis-ease has resulted from just accepting.

This dis-ease occurs when the mind pretends to accept, but the heart chakra remains closed. Yes, we do know about chakras – where did you think the ancients got their knowledge from?

So how do you bridge the gap between the heart and mind? Use the mind. Use the mind to help you understand how the other person's behavior has changed you for the better. Then, rather than turn the other cheek like a martyr, you can move on. This will also help the aggressor to move on, and all will gain.

People do not 'do things' to others so that they can be forgiven, but so that they can understand and bring understanding.

Thank you for helping us spread the understanding.

Blessings to you and yours.

42 PATIENCE PAYS OFF

This message is about patience. As your intuitive ability grows, you get a clearer picture of what the future holds. That is good, because you can then train and focus your thoughts on what is coming, and you can bring it on rather than wait for it.

However, here is the key. That future can only happen when everyone directly involved is ready. Your future never affects only you. You have a contract with everyone else that is involved, and they all need to be as ready as you are. That is where you need to be patient.

And yes, we will never communicate a future to you that will not happen. It is a matter of time and then everyone is ready, and your envisaged future happens in one flowing movement consisting of several small, orchestrated moves.

All you need to do is keep your faith and see your future unfold.

Love and Light to you and yours.

43 YOUR ESSENCE

Goodness, but you grow fast nowadays – and we don't mean physically – we mean spiritually. And the physical world is moving fast with you.

Now the message – and you must please publish these messages.

We want to explain the concept of essence to you – yes, you heard right.

What is your essence? Is it what is left over when everything is stripped away and only you remain?

Yes, there are many theories out there about Love and Light, and especially about Love.

From where we stand, your essence is the smallest spark of energy that comes from you. You never lose it – that spark carries you from one life to another, like an Olympic torch.

You retain the same essence with every life that you live on this earth, and after every life your essence grows. That is why some people have a much larger presence than other people – they have a larger essence.

Why do we say that your essence is more important than Love and Light? Because by using your essence you process energy and create Love and Light. This is no chicken-and-egg.

What can you do to grow your essence?

Just live your life with awareness. Every time you become aware of a special moment – whether you are in it or recall it – your awareness grows. You process that moment and gratitude is created. Your essence grows.

There are hundreds of such small moments in every day. You tend to notice only the big moments. Become aware of the smaller moments as well, and see the effect.

Blessings to you and yours.

44 LOVE YOURSELF

A new day, a new page, a new opportunity.

Our message today is short. Love yourself.

Somehow humanity got the message that it is important to love others –
their neighbors, those who have less and so on, but that self-love is wrong
and a sin.

See self-love as a barrel of fruit juice. If it belongs to you, would you
want to drink it all yourself or share it with others that you care about?
Self-love keeps that barrel full.

Love yourself.

Have a blessed day.

45 INNER PEACE

We bring a message of peace – inner peace.

When you are in a period of transition, inner peace seems to leave you. However, that is not the case.

What happens is that you use your inner peace as a stepping stone for a higher level of inner peace.

Imagine yourself as being surrounded by a large bubble that you feel quite comfortable in. Then you start growing in stature, and you grow to the point where the bubble becomes too small for you.

The bubble does not burst. It becomes your stepping stone. The discomfort arises when you have to balance on this ball while a new, larger bubble grows around you.

It takes time to realize that no balancing act is required. You stand quite solidly on your ball of previous experiences, while a filigreed bubble forms around you.

As the filigree fills in, you get settled.

Your challenge is to be patient and to show Love and kindness to those around you as part of your imaginary balancing act – which becomes real balance as you go along.

Lots of Love to you.

46 MAKING CHOICES

The planets are getting into place. And yes, they have been for millennia and on a large scale. But even a large scale needs precision. The precision is now taking place.

With those planetary movements come a strong healing energy that people can choose to use. Choice will in the next few months be more important than ever when various options unfold.

The options that unfold with our help will all benefit mankind. The 'destructive' choice will be when people choose not to accept any of our options.

Sadly, there is still much ignorance in the world. Distributing our messages helps and you must do it as we deliver them.

Most aware people have made their choices and the earth energy is shifting because of that. Yes, people can influence the earth energy because they have the power – they must just choose to use it.

What did you choose?

Blessings to you and yours.

47 NEW BEGINNINGS

You are counting the days to a new beginning that you know is waiting for you.

We want to give you a new and different view on this.

You are in fact only waiting for the materialization of what is already.

A new beginning does not start when things finally start to happen. Over years you have planted many seeds and seen seeds planted. Those seeds have grown and become young plants. A new beginning means that the young plants are finally bearing fruits.

Everything that eventually happens to you starts with a moment of awareness. When you pinpoint that moment of awareness and write it down, you retain the awareness and see other signposts along the way that quickens the growth process because your faith is strengthened and you make choices in line with the signposts. This becomes a way of life – an alternative education.

You and yours are blessed.

48 JUSTICE

We want to talk to you about justice. When is justice achieved? When an ancient debt is paid.

Yes, you do know it as karma – and it has nothing to do with a judicial system that creates an illusion of its own.

This ancient debt is not paid as an eye for an eye. It is woven into the contracts that you enter into before you enter your physical body.

And no, justice does not mean 'bad' karma. Justice means that you finally get into a position where there is no escape and no choice, and you have to act if you want to go on living.

No, we do not mean you always have to deal with a life-threatening situation. We are talking about making decisions that help you destroy boundaries which stunt your growth on your eternal path.

This justice can take many forms and never has anything to do with the judicial illusion.

But it always has to do with a life crisis.

Think about where justice has been served to you because you had the courage of your heart and acted. That is karma.

We will explain more of this at a later time.

Blessings to you.

49 HOW TO CREATE ABUNDANCE

Today we have an important message to share with you – on how to create abundance.

Abundance of anything you want is easy to create. Think the thought from your heart and then wait. It will happen.

When we say 'think the thought from your heart' we don't mean you should apply your mind – on the contrary. Your mind or brain has nothing to do with this.

See your heart area as a radio receiver. When you think from your heart, it means your heart opens up like a lotus flower and becomes like a 'sponge' for radio signals.

That 'sponge' both sends and receives signals to us and from us. It works in coordination with your third eye and uses the same sense.

This is not a process you can consciously control, no matter what all your gurus teach people.

The process of 'thinking from your heart' is a combination of receiving your destiny and influencing your destiny. It happens all the time. All you need to do is be more aware of what is happening. That helps you make 'better' choices - choices more in line with your heart's desire.

When you think 'from your heart', the thought forms in your consciousness. You already know those thoughts – you call them hunches.

Blessings to you and yours.

50 FORGIVE AND FORGET?

Yes, our connection is always in place.

You have questions about forgiveness, as in 'forgive and forget'.

Yes, forgiveness is about understanding the lesson. Until you have grasped everything at cellular level in your body, you will have resistance. As long as there is resistance, there is no forgiveness.

Do you blame yourself for not having forgiven fully yet? No, never. Keep looking, learning and striving for completion and completeness.

You will have completion when your heart opens like a lotus flower. That is when you embrace your enemy and the word 'enemy' loses its meaning to you, because it loses its emotional context.

Remember that forgiveness does not come within a day or a week. It comes within a moment – the right moment for everyone. It is not something you can fake.

And it is not worth feeling guilty about.

Your plate is full of goodness. Eat from that plate today.

Love and Light to you.

51 POLITICS AND MUD-SLINGING

Let's talk about politics and mud-slinging. Some politicians are such strong spirits that they make themselves targets for the entire planet. People forget these politicians are also human.

52 THE EMERGING WORLD PART 1

The world is in a state of flux, people are unsure, there is mass communication that makes things worse, and the lack of Love is showing in many forms. Religion has taken over and is being exposed every day.

Politicians who are meant to help are exposed as hindrances and power-hungry.

This is a clear path to more chaos, because people are finally standing up to their elected representatives.

Add to that the fact that the planets are constantly shifting, and this impacts on human bodies in a way that the human mind cannot comprehend.

This is quite a journey.

Soon there will be a change in dimensions. Sadly, this will cause more division because those who are unaware will look at those who are aware in envy and fear.

Let's explain the change in dimensions. This is not a mass exodus of souls. It is a change in perception due to a change in consciousness and vibration.

The change in consciousness results in some people opening up and rising above the petty strife of your world. These people will continue to function as they do, but with a lightness of body, mind and spirit. They feel an inclusive Love and rise above prejudice.

They become untouchable and see the world in a different light. They have no ego left. That has always been a strange concept to us – an ego is like a self-absorbent plaster that covers up a 'multitude of sins'. Not that sin exists. This is also not about control. The ego has been a convenient replacement for self-insight and responsibility – you can call it another religion.

When you take away the excuse of 'it's my ego', the person is left with no option than to grow.

That is another term that has nearly become a religion, and also for the wrong reasons.

When we refer to personal growth, we refer to molecular changes that happen at the moment of insight. But more about that later.

53 THE EMERGING WORLD PART 2

Many people will be living in two dimensions. It will not be a matter of those who can looking down on those who can't – on the contrary.

Those who can, already contribute much Love and goodwill to this world and will continue to do so. This will result in much healing to those who can't.

Why is this healing required?

Because people have been poisoned and need to recover from that. We are not only referring to the poisoned food they have been eating. We are also talking about poisonous thoughts that are now being exposed world-wide.

There is a movement of Love and goodwill that is growing by the day. This is countered by a movement of division and destruction that is also growing. This will not result in another world war or something like chemical warfare – there is no time for that.

The result is a change in the thought processes of most people.

Where the change has already taken place, people will surge ahead and create a new world.

This world is being inhabited by free thinkers who are shaking off any remaining limitations. The effect of that is that they are making the world attractive to those people who until now have chosen to live in one dimension.

This division of minds and thoughts is causing much discomfort in the spirit and bodies of the people who until now have chosen to live with bias and poison.

The good news is that over time they will choose to grow into the new world, and this choice will result in better health overall.

Of course, we are also talking about a final revolution in the way health and health care are viewed world-wide.

The poisonous chemical health care will be exposed more and more, and be replaced by the care of consciousness and understanding.

This will also impact on birth rates, because physically deformed bodies will no longer choose the earth as a destination.

Over the next few centuries the population will shrink rather than grow.

Those who still live in one dimension will expect a population growth because of better living conditions, but they will be proven wrong by the figures.

This is a natural process that is evolving as we speak.

54 THE EMERGING WORLD PART 3

The world is healing.

Yes, there is the 'green movement' but that does not have much impact because it is aimed at the wrong people – those who do not care.

No movement or law can make people care.

Either people care from the heart, or they don't. Any official organization makes them care from the mind, and that replaces Love with bureaucracy.

The lungs of the earth are healing. This means that the people are healing and growing towards the Sun and towards one-ness.

And no, that does not mean 'we are all one' – on the contrary.

One-ness refers to the integration of the individual, and to becoming while.

We want to explain this even further to get rid of the clichés.

Becoming whole means becoming more like God – more tolerant, Loving, forgiving, feeling from the heart. It does not mean becoming God – no person has enough past, current and future lives to do that.

One-ness does not mean equality for all. If every person is equal to every other person, the result will be an earth populated by robots.

The biggest proponents of a commercial 'one-ness' are people who do not understand their own composition or purpose, and who as a result borrow form everyone they come into contact with. That is not one-ness. That is neediness.

One-ness does not refer to 'yours is mine, and mine is yours', but rather to a healthy body which reflects a healthy spirit governed or supported by a healthy mind.

Does all of this refer to eating only specific foodstuffs and ignoring others as a matter of principle? No, it refers to being highly attuned and constantly aligning spirit, mind and body in this sequence.

Does that mean eating other living organisms? Of course – no person can live without doing that.

Is there a list of prescribed organisms that are best to eat? Maybe, maybe not. Eat what your body does not reject, and what gives you energy. And eat in moderation – always.

55 THE EMERGING WORLD PART 4

We want to talk more about the state of the world.

Let's talk about your history – and we want for the moment to focus on negativity. Somehow people on earth have managed to capture only the negative parts of history, believing that blood and gore change the world.

We want to assure you that the biggest and most profound changes that ever happened to change the world, were those that happened in the hearts of men in an instant.

And no, that is not a sexist statement. Men have determined the flow of history for millennia while women provided continuity and stability in the background.

Only a few women wandered into male territory and they paid a price much higher than men.

This is also about a male energy disappearing into the background. Yes, there is still much blood and gore, but while the focus is on the visible which is a small part of the Universe, the invisible is taking over.

The feminine energy which is peace-making is growing strongly.

We are not saying the world is moving into a blinding utopia – on the contrary. There is nothing blinding about this development.

As humanity grows and matures, there is more acceptance of each other.

Yes, you have noticed it recently where a man was brutally killed, and instead of a revolution even the calls of those closest to the victim and the perpetrators were for peace and acceptance. This is what the outcome was – a clear indicator of how people accept each other rather than make war.

56 THE EMERGING WORLD PART 5

We have so much to say about what lies ahead. We want people to be ready and to understand what they are getting into. Many people will find it both interesting and frustrating to live in a physical world with two dimensions as well as a non-physical dimension. Most people will find that scary and hard to understand, and will simply switch off the higher physical dimension and choose to live in fear.

Let us explain more.

Most people live in a dimension where fear and duality rules. They read the newspaper and absorb other media that aims at sensation and misinformation. They choose to accept what is given to them by those they deem to be superior, and they accept the energy that is sent to them.

Now add another dimension that some people are more aware of than others. This is the invisible dimension of dreams, inspiration and creativity where wisdom comes from.

Now add a third dimension to this, namely a physical dimension that is very visible, where there is no place for fear and much place for abundance and freedom and an all-encompassing brotherly love. This dimension has always existed, but is now being populated by means of people who have finally reached a stage of self-acceptance and God-acceptance.

This is a dimension that the 'two-dimensional' people look up to with adoration and envy, not realizing how close they are to entering this third dimension. This is the main task of the 'three-dimensional' people – to reach down and help others understand and neutralize their fear, so that they can grow and evolve into this third dimension.

Their biggest fear is the fear of losing those they love, and that holds them back. They don't realize they simply open a new door, walk through and then hold the door open to their loved ones to follow them. They see the transition as a moment of loss, because they are stuck in the one-dimensional fear of death. This is a personal Mount Everest even for those who claim to be aware of the continuum of life from death to life to eternity.

58 THE EMERGING WORLD PART 6

We were explaining the different levels of society that are emerging – in fact, one additional level is emerging.

There is already a number of true new movements related to this new emerging way of life. Much of it is a reflection of pure thinking that is eliminating and exposing old and dishonest or unethical practices. These new movements all reflect the purity of thought that is typical of the new breed of human – persistent in no longer accepting an illusion that has false foundations.

However, there are some existing movements that have on the surface all the hallmarks of the new movements, but these false movements do not stand up to scrutiny.

We are referring to a number of so-called charities that are most uncharitable in their practices. These movements have a solid capitalistic basis even though their public images are the opposite.

Over the next decade each one of these movements will be exposed for what they truly are. The basis for this exposure is that the leaders of these movements are unable to keep up the façade.

Their hearts and minds are out of sync, and they get tired of being in two places. As a result, they show their weaknesses and are unable to cover up.

When this exposure happens, while the rest of the world is baying for blood, the true new movements step in and show the solid foundation based on Love.

These are not altruistic movements based on a 'one for all and all for one' philosophy, but rather movements run by like-minded people who simply do what resonates with them on a basis that brings followers who agree.

There will always be leaders and followers. However, this new breed of followers is not slaves of fear, but rather evolving beings who are attracted by the next higher vibration on their path.

With the true new movements there is no fear, and there is no rank. There is a true magnetic power where like attracts like.

From the outside there may be the appearance of rank, but from the inside there is clear equality of purpose and differentiation of level of involvement.

This is like the difference between the proverbial chalk and cheese. In the old movements, all followers are chalk soldiers and that is what they remain.

In the new movement, the followers are like different strengths of cheese, and all is still evolving.

58 THE EMERGING WORLD PART 7

As we explained, life on earth is becoming three-dimensional. A large group of people is moving up the evolution ladder to live in this higher dimension. Sadly, an even larger group is still resisting.

The difference will become clearer over time. There will be those who struggle with e-motion on a daily basis, and those who radiate peace and tranquility.

Some of those who strive towards the higher state will get to recognize it but not feel it in their hearts. They will apply their minds and make themselves believe that they are part of 'the chosen'. Not only is there no such thing as 'the chosen', but these deluded people will create their own reality of confusion.

You will still in your lifetime see the symptoms of division and delusion, and it will be very sad. It will be like seeing a group of people saying 'Look at me – I can dance' while they stumble around and get in the way of gracious dancers.

Recognizing clarity and purity is far from living it.

An entire new generation of children are being born with abilities that will make them rebel against systems and paradigms in the gentlest but firmest way.

They will not only question many ancient traditions based on falsehood, but revive other ancient traditions effortlessly and create a new world on earth. These children will grow up to see things like pollution and radiation disappear by dissolving them with the power of their mind.

They are already achieving much in terms of health by puzzling doctors with their ability to heal not only themselves but those they get into contact with.

You ask why these children need healing in the first place? They absorb a lot of 'black energy' as part of a cleansing process and they experience strong symptoms of poisoning expressed as cancer.

The good news is that these children are aware of their task of 'sifting' their environment and they work consciously on clearing their bodies once they have absorbed the energy that needs clearing

59 THE EMERGING WORLD PART 8

The change in awareness that we have described is already taking place. The biggest change is in the perception of the younger generation. They see through all the dishonesty and deception around them.

They are confused – not because they don't know what to do, but because they don't understand how the older generation can just accept many things that are not true or clear.

This is part of the growing change in consciousness and awareness.

ABOUT THE AUTHOR

Elsabe Smit is a well-known international coach, facilitator, author, and public speaker that uses her clairvoyant and intuitive skills in her daily life to assist all of those that she comes into contact with in her professional life.

She has an MBA (Master Business Administration), a MA in Industrial Psychology, and extensive experience as a Business Analyst. Using all her knowledge, skills and competencies, Elsabe helps people to understand the mysteries of life and Love, so that they can regain control of their lives.

Elsabe Smit was born and raised in South Africa, but has since 2000 been living in the UK.

After years of facing numerous personal challenges, involving her relationship with her drug- and alcohol-addicted mother, living with and getting divorced from an abusive husband, being a single mother, being a mistress for a period of time, and then facing unemployment, she one day realized that she had been given the amazing gift of intuition and clairvoyance.

Using her newly discovered gifts, she then rediscovered herself. She learned that all her past experiences, "good" and "bad", were only stepping stones on her life's blueprint towards loving and accepting herself.

Having always having had a keen interest in human behavior, this discovery took her on a different path, adding the study of life, death and spirituality to her interests. During that journey, she explored NLP and embraced Quantum Physics. Elsabe studied some of the world's best acknowledged researchers and gurus in the fields of relationships, health and business.

During her professional life, Elsabe's career included lecturing at a South African University, being a Human Resources Manager with a mining house and a multinational security firm, and being a freelance business analyst.

In between the various permanent positions and contracts, she developed her reputation as a sought-after author, speaker, facilitator, coach and mentor.

As an author, some of her books are today still in use as prescribed text books for university and college students in South Africa. Other books have been published and are available on Amazon, and some books have been published on her website as E-books which she shares as free gifts.

As a speaker, facilitator and trainer she has presented numerous programs to groups ranging from a dozen to hundreds of people. The subject matter has been as varied and interesting as her life.

As a mentor, she coached and mentored small business owners, blue-chip executives and employees covering a myriad of professions, employment levels and industries.

Don't forget her contribution to the world of psychics. She's been on various radio and TV shows with international audiences. In addition, Elsabe has done thousands of personal psychic readings for people from all walks of life located in more than 80 countries - including one for a death row inmate in a US prison.

Throughout her life, Elsabe has been passionately focused on identifying the nuances that make a difference in people lives, the why's of birth, life and death - and now it's your turn to tap into the vast wealth of knowledge and experiences that she has gained during her lifetime, so that like Elsabe ...

YOU can also Discover yourself and Love YOUR Life.

If you have questions, or comments, contact Elsabe at elsabe@elsabesmit.com, or visit her website at www.elsabesmit.com to access her skill so that you can resolve your burning issue.

You can also follow Elsabe on Twitter or LinkedIn or YouTube or Google+

Are you stuck in a relationship that has reached a dead end?

Is a past relationship still haunting you?

Then you have come to the right place!

This book will quickly give you a new perspective and help you to move on and have a happy life. The book will show you how your current or past partner has helped you learn about yourself. You will recover from any relationship and feel very good about yourself.

Make a small investment in your future happiness, and you will receive answers and solutions that will make your heart sing again.

Here is what the book can do for you:

- Help you understand the purpose of your relationship.
- Explain how your partner thinks.
- Define true Love and why it is so elusive.
- Find your motive for staying in a destructive relationship
- Provide a step by step solution for ending the relationship.
- Take away your guilt and resentment.
- Help you discover the value in any relationship - even a bad one.
- Stop those nightmares and sleepless nights.
- Explain why it is OK for your relationship to end.
- Discover why you have stayed in a destructive relationship until now.
- Explain the true meaning of gratitude.

- Discover how gratitude releases you from your relationship.
- Give you a vision of your future.
- Show you how to find the strength to move on.
- Teach you to Love the face in your mirror again.

This is what readers have said about the book:

"You can feel the compassion in her words, how awesome is that. Thank you so much for such a wonderful, positive response."

"Thank you so much for the help, my dear friend. I could say thanks you a million times or at least in several different languages but it still wouldn't get the point across. Thank you."

"That makes a lot of sense. I'm going to sit down and talk with him tonight and see where we stand as for the wedding. I love him and we'll make it work no matter what. Thanks."

"Makes perfect sense!"

"Recently I have had Elsabe's wisdom and experience on ending a relationship. I must admit I have never ended a relationship without feeling guilt, remorse or a sense of devastation, but this time Elsabe helped me to see that the relationship had come to its natural end and I was able to let go and move on with love in my heart for my ex-partner and no feeling of having to make amends or justify my actions. My ex-partner has let me go too. WE came to a mutual understanding that we had some wonderful times together and that we had both seen positive changes happen in each other over the years we were together. Elsabe has helped me accept that relationships don't last forever and once we they have served their purpose there is only pain if we chose to hang on to them 'past their sell by date'. I feel remarkably different now like a weight has been lifted. Thank you, Elsabe, for your valuable time wisdom and insight. Your message is one which I know others will be blessed to hear."

Search for the book on your local Amazon website, or contact the author on www.ElsabeSmit.com to order a signed copy.

Have you always wanted to understand how energy healing works?

Is energy healing the placebo effect in a different form?

This book conveys a powerful promise early on and then delivers on this promise throughout the material:

"Every physical illness and dis-ease stems from a disturbance in the rhythm of time. We will go back to the disturbance and allow time to flow freely. This will then remove the energy block and this is where the healing takes place."

The book gives a different perspective on the age-old question of why God allows suffering and claims to be a God of Love:

"God only creates that which is beyond time and space. People then distil from God's creation and add their own details, and they fall back on their indoctrination to pass the credit as well as the blame for the creation of their own making on to God."

This book explains how healing empowers people:

"...people get an understanding of their own creative powers. They understand that they have created the dis-ease. They understand that they create the cure. They understand the difference between their own creative powers and the creative powers of God. Most important, they gain an understanding of a loving God."

Healing is explained as undoing the behavior that caused the dis-ease, then undoing the dis-ease, and then re-doing the behavior without the dis-ease, so that the person can consciously change their behavior and not fall back into the toxic patterns that resulted from the original injury.

The author of the book warns that energy healing is not necessarily about extending this physical life:

"At all times the focus of healing is to remove the energy blockage and to provide a belief system that will allow the person to continue on the journey."

This healing is truly holistic.

"We do not just heal the symptoms, because when we do that, the behavior pattern will remain and the damage will be repeated, often on an even larger scale. We remove the energy blockage, and at the same time we do deep healing work on the spirit."

There are several powerful comments that shed a new light on beliefs and physical conditions e.g. obesity:

"The whole purpose of religion is to make people weak and to ensure that they are malleable, in other words to suck out their energy and replace it with a Void that they feel as long as they are in the power of religion. Obese people fill that Void with food and drink."

There is a lot more in this book than just the extracts above.

Search for the book on your local Amazon website, or contact the author on www.ElsabeSmit.com to order a signed copy.

In this enlightening book, internationally renowned psychic, coach and author Elsabe Smit breaks down some key concepts of spiritual development into short, highly accessible articles, and provides ways in which the reader can achieve spiritual growth.

Inspired by a lifetime of facing sometimes seemingly insurmountable challenges, Elsabe examines the subtle nuances that influence our lives, and explores these age-old questions: Why are we born? How can we get closer to enlightenment? Is there life after death?

Drawing on elements of quantum physics, plus works by some of the world's most prominent researchers and gurus in the fields of health, business and relationships, Elsabe will help you to understand the ancient mystery of Love.

She will help you to regain control of your life and, using spiritual concepts, find enlightenment in life's daily challenges.

All life experiences, whether you label them as 'good' or 'bad', are simply stepping stones on a journey towards finding self-acceptance, compassion and your own spirituality.

In this highly practical guide to modern day spirituality, Elsabe shares her life experiences and wealth of knowledge gained over many years both on this plane and in psychic work.

Elsabe will show you how to discover your true self and to appreciate the life you have been given.

In "*Spiritual Growth: How to Strengthen Your Faith and Spirituality (The Enlightenment Series Volume 1)*" you will get answers to these questions:

- Where do I find solace?
- How can I improve my karma?
- Why do we experience the dark night of the soul and how can we get through it?
- How do we match our expectations to the outcomes we get?
- What is the true meaning of time and numbers?
- Does faith require trust and belief?
- How do the risks we take strengthen our faith?
- How do you celebrate your beliefs?
- Did you know that clinging to the wrong idea can affect your health?
- Why is it important to live every day, not just Sundays, as part of your faith?
- How can the Law of Attraction give you the opposite of what you want?
- How do you have to explore your Awareness and find your spiritual teacher?
- How do you deal with tough decisions about injustice to others?
- How to practice detachment and improve your own judgement
- How to find the gain from dealing with grief and death
- How to identify and eliminate your self-imposed labels and boundaries
- Why should older people be respected?
- Who is your neighbour and how should you love your neighbour?
- How can you deal with prejudice?
- Why does the church discriminate against gay people and females?

The book is written as a series of short articles with useful prompts throughout that encourage you to pause and reflect, make notes, answer questions and complete exercises.

Search for the book on your local Amazon website, or contact the author on www.ElsabeSmit.com to order a signed copy.

Do you tend to make snap judgments about others and jump to conclusions?

Do you blame people for the experiences you have?

Have you noticed how people display their emotional intelligence and wondered if you do the same?

Then this book is for you.

Elsabe explains how our emotions cloud our judgement and get us into trouble.

"Improve Your Emotional Intelligence: The Spiritual Development of Your Emotions (The Enlightenment Series Volume 2)" is not about blame or guilt, or other time-wasting uses of energy. The book is about explaining how we can manage and use our emotions in our favor. Imagine being in charge of every situation because you are in a space of calmness and in control.

Yes, life is a challenge. That is what we are here for. We can allow our emotions to run away with us and make situations worse, or we can understand how emotions work and use them in our favor.

Elsabe is a well-known psychic, author and coach. She has a unique view on life based on information she channeled through psychic readings and dreams. Elsabe then applied that information to her own life and gained more wisdom.

This book is *one in a series of books* where she shares her wisdom in a simple, effective way by allowing her readers to share her journey.

This book will teach you:

- How to define yourself by changing your mood and emotions.
- Why your strong emotions push people away from you and how you can change those emotions in your favor
- How to respect the inner pain of others without judging
- How you can change the world one step at a time by starting with your own life
- Why we have family strife but we remain family
- How we make things worse with emotional outbursts and jumping to conclusions
- That you can add to issues in the news e.g. crime by focusing your thoughts on them, or you can choose what you want to focus on
- How a bad temper can make you do stupid things and how you can take ownership and become more spiritual
- A way of changing a wrong first impression by looking for the good in the person
- That when you recognize your own worth, bullies cannot bother you
- How lies can shape an entire future for the people involved
- Why inner peace does not last but contributes to spiritual development
- How to turn other people's views about you into emotional intelligence
- That memories are there to be cherished, and they are part of your enlightenment
- Why happiness comes from inside and not from other people
- That a focus on positive thinking does a lot more damage than accepting life's ups and downs
- How powerful forgiveness can be in your life
- That memories become part of us and it is up to us to own and love them
- How to practice the universal law of "say what you do and do what you say"

The book is written as a series of short articles with useful prompts throughout that encourage you to pause and reflect, make notes, answer questions and complete exercises.

Search for the book on your local Amazon website, or contact the author on www.ElsabeSmit.com to order a signed copy.

In this enlightening book, internationally renowned psychic and author Elsabe Smit breaks down some key concepts of spiritual development into short, highly accessible articles, and provides ways in which you can find spiritual meaning in your daily life. She questions mundane experiences and finds the practical meaning of spirit in this age of enlightenment.

All experiences, whether you label them as 'good' or 'bad', are simply stepping stones on a journey towards finding self-acceptance and compassion in this age of enlightenment.

Elsabe will show you how to discover spiritual meaning and appreciate your life.

In *"More of Life's Questions: Find Your Moment of Revelation (The Enlightenment Series Vol 3)"* you will find enlightenment and define your own spirituality with these questions:

How to respect religion and religious boundaries even if you are not religious

How the flow of energy impacts on our relationships

How we set boundaries for ourselves and delay our own enlightenment experiences

How the creation process works and how we can use that to find spiritual meaning

How to find your way through life with pen and paper rather than expensive therapy by using the most potent journaling method known.

And many other questions.

The book is written as a series of short articles with useful prompts throughout that encourage you to pause and reflect, make notes, answer questions and complete exercises. By the end of this book you will define spirituality in your own way an understand what enlightenment is about.

Search for the book on your local Amazon website, or contact the author on www.ElsabeSmit.com to order a signed copy.

Inspirational daily quotes for each day of the year to encourage spiritual growth and explain why certain events happen in your life

Ask yourself the following:

- Do you notice the small miracles in your life?
- Do you see the truth in mundane events?
- Do you like to start your day with a spiritual pick-me-up?

If you answered YES to the above, then this book is for you.

Elsabe Smit has a knack for bringing spiritual teaching into our lives by interpreting events. She sees the truth in small things and brings them in line with the spiritual teachings that are sometimes hard to put into practice.

In this book she shares her wisdom in a simple, effective way by providing snippets for contemplation.

In *"Wonder Why? Inspirational Daily Quotes for All Ages"* you will learn:

- How your perceptions influence your experience
- Why having strong emotions about anything makes your life worse
- How to use humor that bites like a lamb rather than a lion
- That under the skin we all share the same life experiences
- How tradition sometimes is based on wrong information
- Why carrying grudges is not healthy
- That life and the Universe aims at helping us find balance
- What energy is and how to use energy

- How to get the best out of change
- How to turn incidents into opportunities

And many other themes …

The book is written as a series of inspirational daily quotes on which you can pause and reflect every day.

Search for the book on your local Amazon website, or contact the author on www.ElsabeSmit.com to order a signed copy.

If you discovered this book because you were looking for chocolate recipes, then there was some divine intervention.

It is possible that your soul is starving for some inspiring, non-fattening soul chocolate.

Dip into this book daily to get some inspiration and sustenance, and help you focus on your own truth. Find meaning in simple things and add soul music to your life.

All you need to do is open this book on any page, and you have a focus for your **daily meditation**, providing **sustenance for your soul**.

Search for the book on your local Amazon website, or contact the author on www.ElsabeSmit.com to order a signed copy.

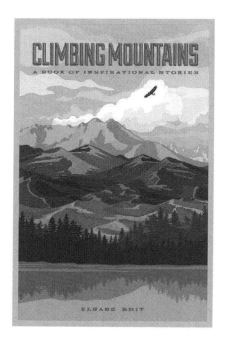

Have you ever experienced a definitive moment that shaped your life and determined your future?

Have you observed the actions of a loved one and asked yourself why they acted as they did?

Did you ever experience a true light-bulb moment that has stayed with you ever since?

Do you sometimes feel as if you are the only person on this planet who had a mind-blowing experience?

Or do you like to read about the lives of other people to help you make sense of your own experiences?

Then this book is for you.

The book contains short inspirational stories about life. Each story deals with a different theme, indicating the motivation behind the actions of the people involved, and how they were inspired in various ways, for example insights into their choices that brought them peace of mind, or a moment of inspiration after having an out-of-this-world experience.

The stories make you think about your own situation and how you can be inspired to new insights.

Search for the book on your local Amazon website, or contact the author on www.ElsabeSmit.com to order a signed copy.

RESILIENCE

How to conquer the
fear and challenges
of self-employment

Fraser J. Hay   Elsabe Smit

If you would like to experience the practical application of Elsabe's wisdom, get yourself a copy of the book *"Resilience: How to Conquer the Fears and Challenges of Self-Employment."*

Self-Employed? Ever felt frustrated, isolated - even desperate on occasion with no-one to turn to for help, guidance or support? If so, then this powerful, practical book will help you to keep moving forwards and living your dream.

Ask yourself the following questions:

- How do you take your business from brain to heart to stellar?
- Where does forgiveness feature in your business plan?
- Why do bad things happen to good people, despite their best intentions?
- What if the business idea you have put your heart and soul into goes wrong?
- Who do you turn to for advice and how can you keep on track in the face of adversity?

The powerful, proven, practical and highly effective concepts, techniques, and spiritual principles in this book can be applied to almost every commercial problem, issue or challenge that you will face in starting and running your own business.

Real world, practical examples and exercises are included for you to personalize and apply to your current circumstances.

Ever been anxious, frustrated or worried about:

- What makes you really "different" or unique in your marketplace?
- Deciding and accepting what you really offer potential customers?
- Finding, winning and keeping Customers?

- Charging (and getting paid) what you're really worth?
- Juggling home life with running a business?
- Making the right decision at the right time?
- Getting paid for work already done?
- Personal and professional conflict?
- Allowing your fears to prevent you from achieving your goals?
- Dealing with the emotional stress of starting and running your own business?
- Learning to know, like and trust yourself?

"Resilience: How to Conquer the Fears and Challenges of Self-Employment" shares a common-sense approach that simply isn't common practice among the millions of self-employed facing the daily issues, challenges & obstacles of self-employment that are holding them back and preventing them from achieving their personal, professional and commercial goals and objectives.

Discover:

- How to make sense of conflict - since you cannot avoid it
- How to turn rejection into opportunity
- When do you celebrate success and when to navigate hurdles for even greater success
- Where to find inspired answers and solutions
- How you can prepare for meetings knowing the outcome in advance
- When to walk away and when to fight back, and why
- What the real "lessons" are that you need to master, to guarantee your personal success
- How to reassure yourself, your family or your loved ones that you're mentally prepared for the challenges presented to you, your finances or your health

You want to work for yourself and you want to be in control of your own destiny. We know it, you know it and your heart knows it! Do you want to live the life and lifestyle you've always craved?

You've already got the power and resilience to succeed in self-employment.

You just need to recognize it, and be shown how to use it.

Search for the book on your local Amazon website, or contact the author on www.ElsabeSmit.com to order a signed copy.

ONE LAST THING ...

If you believe the book is worth sharing, please would you take a few seconds to leave a review on Amazon and let your friends know about it? If it turns out to make a difference in their lives, they'll be forever grateful to you, as will I.

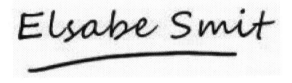

Made in the USA
Columbia, SC
02 February 2020